Wrap of the Week

52 Quick and Easy Wrap Recipes for Healthy Weight Loss

Lucy Fast

Just to say Thank You for Purchasing this Book I want to give you a gift 100% absolutely FREE

A Copy of My Upcoming Special Report
"Paleo Pantry: The Beginner's Guide to What Should and Should NOT be in Your Paleo Kitchen"

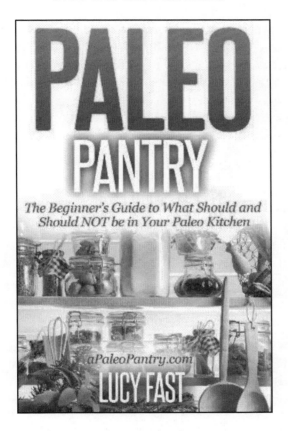

Go to www.aPaleoPantry.com
to Reserve Your FREE Copy

Table of Contents

Wrap of the Week

Introduction

What is a wrap?

A wrap is simply a sandwich that is made with flexible flatbread, such as tortillas, pitas or lavash, rolled around filling, which usually consists of meats, vegetables, cheeses and sauces. It is different from a sandwich in the sense that the latter is made from two different layers of bread that hold the filling in place, while the former has only one layer that completely surrounds the filling.

Although it has existed for quite some time, the wrap has quickly gained popularity not only as a snack choice, but also as a convenient lunch item. Most wraps are incredibly easy and convenient to make, serve and enjoy. They do not require a large spread and can even be eaten on the go. Most wrap recipes are also flexible enough to contain a variety of ingredients from different cuisines. Moreover, wraps make it much easier to control food portions compared to full-size meals.

A brief history of wraps

People from different parts of the world, including Mexico, Northern America, Greece, Western Asia and Turkey, have been making wraps since the late 1800s. In its western form, it is widely believed that the wrap was invented by a southern Californian restaurant chain called "I Love Juicy" in the 1980s. However, Bobby Valentine also claims to have invented the wrap in his Stamford, Connecticut café at approximately the same time.

Despite the disagreement on its origins however, it is undisputed that the wrap has steadily gained popularity in the west in the 1990s. Today, it is now served in a number of popular restaurant chains, such as KFC, McDonald's, Subway, Chick-fil-A, Roly Poly, Sonic Drive-In and more.

Why make your own wraps?

Like many sandwiches, the quality of wraps can vary wildly from boring to exciting, bland to flavorful. One of the chief reasons for this is because we habitually consume the same or relatively similar sandwiches. But how do we break out of this monotony? By expanding our repertoire of recipes.

Aside from improving the overall taste and quality of your meals, another advantage of making your own wraps is that you'll get to save significantly more money compared to ordering out.

There are quite a few classic sandwiches that you probably already know about, such as Peanut Butter and Jelly, Ham and Cheese or Bacon Lettuce and Tomatoes, so this cookbook will attempt to present a collection of recipes that you may not have tried or twists and variations on the old favorites.

A word of caution

Just because a sandwich is made at home, doesn't make it healthy. As obvious as this may sound, you shouldn't go crazy on ingredients that may not be good for you. Keep your filings as natural as you can and try to avoid processed foods whenever possible. The recipes in this collection do not have a specific dietary restriction. As such, some of the recipes may have been chosen based on their taste and flavor rather than their actual health and nutritional value.

However, this does not in any way mean that you cannot alter the recipe to better fit your body's needs and your personal health goals.

Happy Health Eating!

Lucy Fast

Spring Wraps

California Veggie Wraps
Nutritional Information: Calories 535, Fat 28 g.,
Carbohydrates 55 g., Protein 14 g.
Serves 1

Ingredients:

1 tortilla wrap, warm
1 tbsp. cream cheese, softened
2 tbsp. onion, chopped
2 tbsp. carrot, shredded
2 tbsp. red pepper, sliced
1/4 c. alfalfa sprouts
1/4 c. baby spinach, shredded
1/4 c. cheddar cheese, shredded
1/4 avocado, peeled, sliced
Salt and black pepper to taste

Directions:

1. Place the tortilla on a clean working surface.
2. Spread cream cheese onto the tortilla.
3. Top with the remaining ingredients.
4. Roll, slice and serve.

Southwestern Club Wraps

Nutritional Information: Calories 678, Fat 36 g., Carbohydrates 49 g., Protein 36 g.
Serves 4

Ingredients:

> 1/3 c. barbecue sauce
> 3/4 c. ranch dressing
> 4 tortilla wraps, warm
> 1/2 c. cherry tomatoes, quartered
> 1 c. bell peppers, chopped
> 1 c. black olives, pitted, chopped
> 1/2 lb. turkey, smoked, sliced
> 1/2 lb. Monterey Jack cheese, grated
> 1/4 head iceberg lettuce, sliced
> 1 avocado, peeled, pitted, sliced

Directions:

1. Stir together the first two ingredients in a bowl. Set aside.
2. Place the tortillas on a clean working surface.
3. Spread the prepared mixture onto the tortillas.
4. Top with the remaining ingredients.
5. Roll, slice and serve.

California Sushi Wraps

Nutritional Information: Calories 471, Fat 2 g.,
Carbohydrates 98 g., Protein 13 g.
Serves 4

Ingredients:

> 1/2 tsp. salt
> 2 tbsp. vinegar, rice wine
> 1/4 c. green onion, chopped
> 2 c. sushi rice, cooked
> 4 tortilla wraps, warm
> 2 c. baby spinach
> 1/2 c. carrot, grated
> 1 cucumber, peeled, seeded, sliced into spears
> 8 oz. imitation crabmeat
> Soy sauce to serve

Directions:

1. Stir together the first four ingredients in a bowl. Set aside.
2. Place a tortilla wrap on a clean working surface.
3. Top with 1/2 c. spinach, followed by some of the rice mixture and carrot.
4. Place cucumber spears and crabmeat on one side of the tortilla.
5. Starting on that side, beginning rolling the wrap. Tuck in the open ends.
6. Cover with plastic wrap.
7. Repeat until you use up all the ingredients.
8. Let refrigerate for a few hours.
9. Slice and serve fresh with soy sauce.

Sun-Dried Tomato Veggie Wraps

Nutritional Information: Calories 296, Fat 21 g.,
Carbohydrates 23 g., Protein 7 g.
Serves 4

Ingredients:

> 4 tortilla wraps, warm
> 4 tbsp. cream cheese, whipped
> 1 c. sun-dried tomatoes in oil
> 4 c. baby spinach
> 1 yellow bell pepper, diced
> 2 avocados, peeled, pitted, sliced
> Salt and black pepper to taste

Directions:

1. Place the tortilla wraps on a clean working surface.
2. Spread cream cheese on the tortillas.
3. Top with the remaining ingredients.
4. Roll and tuck in the ends.
5. Slice and serve.

Salmon and Egg Wraps with Mustard-Mayonnaise

Nutritional Information: Calories 356, Fat 15 g.,
Carbohydrates 35 g., Protein 23 g.
Serves 12

Ingredients:

6 tbsp. mustard, Dijon
7 oz. mayonnaise, light
1 red onion, sliced
12 tortilla wraps
7 oz. baby spinach
6 eggs, hardboiled, cooled, shelled, sliced
24 slices salmon, smoked

Directions:

1. Stir together the first two ingredients in a bowl.
2. Divide the mixture into two equal portions.
3. Stir the onion into one portion.
4. Place the tortilla wraps on a clean working surface.
5. Spread the onion mixture onto the tortillas.
6. Top with the remaining ingredients.
7. Roll, slice and serve.

Rice and Bean Enchiladas

Nutritional Information: Calories 634, Fat 13 g.,
Carbohydrates 104 g., Protein 31 g.
Serves 2

Ingredients:

1 tsp. Cajun seasoning
7 oz. rice, cooked
1 bunch spring onions, chopped
2 tortilla wraps
14 oz. refried beans, canned
7 oz. tomato salsa
7 oz. yogurt, fat-free
1 oz. cheddar cheese, grated

Directions:

1. Stir together the first three ingredients in a bowl. Set aside.
2. Preheat an oven to 350 degrees F.
3. Place the tortillas on a clean working surface.
4. Top with refried beans and the prepared rice.
5. Roll and tuck in the ends.
6. Place half the salsa on a baking dish.
7. Place the rolls into the baking dish.
8. Top with half the yogurt and all the cheese.
9. Bake for 30 minutes.
10. Let cool for five minutes.
11. Serve with the remaining yogurt and salsa.

Smoked Trout, Beetroot and Horseradish Wraps

Nutritional Information: Calories 327, Fat 10 g.,
Carbohydrates 42 g., Protein 21 g.
Serves 4

Ingredients:

1 bunch dill
4 slices flatbread
Olive oil as needed
2 tbsp. horseradish, creamed
2 tbsp. crème fraiche
1 squeeze lemon juice
1 pinch lemon zest
Salt and black pepper to taste
3 beetroot, cooked, sliced
4 trout fillets, smoked, broken up
Salad leaves to serve

Directions:

1. Chop half the dill and pick the other half into small fronds.
2. Preheat an oven to 350 degrees F.
3. Coat the flatbread with olive oil.
4. Place the bread on a baking sheet.
5. Bake for eight minutes.
6. While waiting, stir together the next five ingredients in a bowl. Add water if necessary. Set aside.
7. Place the toasted flatbread on a clean working surface.
8. Top with the next two ingredients.
9. Drizzle on the prepared sauce.
10. Wrap and serve with salad leaves.

Asparagus, Carrot and Humus Wraps
Nutritional Information: Calories 355, Fat 19 g.,
Carbohydrates 37 g., Protein 10 g.
Serves 4

Ingredients:

> 4 tortilla wraps, warm
> 7 oz. humus
> 1 handful arugula leaves
> 4 carrots, grated coarsely
> 4 asparagus spears, steamed
> Salt and black pepper to taste

Directions:

1. Place the tortilla wraps on a clean working surface.
2. Spread humus on the tortillas.
3. Top with the remaining ingredients.
4. Roll and serve immediately.

Fresh Tuna Tortillas

Nutritional Information: Calories 370, Fat 15 g.,
Carbohydrates 36 g., Protein 27 g.
Serves 4

Ingredients:

2 tuna steaks
1 tbsp. sunflower oil
1 tsp. cumin, ground
1 pinch cayenne pepper
Salt to taste
4 tortilla wraps, warm
1 handful cilantro, chopped
1 lime, juiced
1 avocado, peeled, pitted, sliced
2 tomatoes, sliced
Sour cream to serve

Directions:

1. Preheat a griddle pan.
2. Coat each tuna steak with sunflower oil.
3. Season with the next three ingredients.
4. Cook the steaks for two minutes each side. Slice into strips.
5. Place the tortilla wraps on a clean working surface.
6. Top with the remaining ingredients.
7. Roll and serve with sour cream.

Smoked Salmon Rotollos

Nutritional Information: Calories 100, Fat 7 g.,
Carbohydrates 5g., Protein 5 g.
Serves 25

Ingredients:

1 tbsp. lemon juice
2 tbsp. dill, chopped
7 oz. cream cheese
1 pinch black pepper
4 tortilla wraps, warm
7 oz. salmon, smoked, sliced

Directions:

1. Stir together the first four ingredients.
2. Place the tortilla wraps on a clean working surface.
3. Spread the resulting mixture on the tortillas.
4. Top with salmon slices.
5. Roll the tortillas like Swiss rolls. Remove the ends.
6. Cover tightly with cling film. Twist the ends to secure.
7. Refrigerate until ready to serve.
8. Slice diagonally before serving.

Barbecued Vegetables with Goat Cheese

Nutritional Information: Calories 415, Fat 26 g.,
Carbohydrates 36 g., Protein 10 g.
Serves 8

Ingredients:

2 bunches spring onions, trimmed
4 small eggplant, slice into 1/2 inch strips
16 asparagus spears
2 tbsp. vinegar, white wine
1/2 c. olive oil
3 cloves garlic, crushed
Salt and black pepper to taste
7 oz. goat cheese, crumbled
1 handful basil leaves
Additional olive oil as needed
8 tortilla wraps

Directions:

1. Place the first three ingredients onto a shallow dish.
2. Whisk together the next four ingredients in a separate bowl.
3. Pour the second mixture into the first. Toss to coat evenly.
4. Preheat a grill to medium-high. (*Note – this can be done in the oven with your broiler, or in a grill pan, if you don't have a grill*)
5. Barbecue the eggplant slices for five minutes each side. Set aside.
6. Barbecue the asparagus and spring onions for three minutes each side. Set aside.
7. Place the barbecued vegetables into a bowl.
8. Add the next three ingredients. Toss to coat evenly. Set aside.

9. Barbecue the tortilla wraps for one minute each side.
10. Place the tortilla wraps on a clean working surface.
11. Top the tortillas with the vegetable mixture.
12. Roll and serve.

Salsa Chicken and Cheese Tortillas

Nutritional Information: Calories 533, Fat 29 g.,
Carbohydrates 44 g., Protein 27 g.
Serves 2

Ingredients:

2 tortilla wraps, warm
4 tbsp. salsa
2 tbsp. cilantro, chopped
1/4 c. leftover chicken, roasted, shredded
1/3 c. cheddar cheese, grated
7 oz. kidney beans, canned, drained, mashed
1 spring onion, chopped
Vegetable oil as needed

Directions:

1. Place the tortilla wraps on a clean working surface.
2. Spread salsa onto the tortillas.
3. Top with the remaining ingredients.
4. Fold to cover the filling.
5. Lightly coat one side of the tortillas with vegetable oil.
6. Place oil-side down on a skillet.
7. Place the skillet over a stove set on medium.
8. Let cook for four minutes.
9. Lightly coat the other side with vegetable oil.
10. Flip over and cook for another two minutes.
11. Slice into wedges and serve.

Taco-Salad Wraps

Nutritional Information: Calories 398, Fat 10 g.,
Carbohydrates 58 g., Protein 23 g.
Serves 6

Ingredients:

1/4 tsp. chili powder
1/2 tsp. salt
1 tsp. cumin, ground
2 tsp. olive oil
15 oz. black beans, canned, rinsed, drained
6 tortilla wraps, warm
1 c. cheddar cheese, grated
3 plum tomatoes, deseeded, diced
6 lettuce leaves

Directions:

1. Mash together the first five ingredients in a bowl. Set aside.
2. Place the tortilla wraps on a clean working surface.
3. Spread the prepared mixture onto the tortillas.
4. Top with the remaining ingredients.
5. Roll, slice and serve.

Summer Wraps

Grilled Zucchini, Bean and Cheese Quesadillas

Nutritional Information: Calories 509, Fat 20 g.,
Carbohydrates 56 g., Protein 23 g.
Serves 4

Ingredients:

> 4 tsp. olive oil
> 1 onion, chopped
> 2 tsp. cumin, ground
> 4 cloves garlic, chopped
> 1 tbsp. tomato puree
> 2 tbsp. water
> 7 oz. pinto beans, canned, drained, rinsed
> Salt and black pepper to taste
> 3 zucchini, sliced diagonally
> 7 oz. cheddar cheese, grated
> 1 handful cilantro, chopped
> 1 green chili, chopped
> 8 tortilla wraps, warm

Directions:

1. Pour half the olive oil into a skillet.
2. Place the skillet over a stove set on medium.
3. Sauté the onion until tender.
4. Add the next two ingredients. Continue to sauté for another minute.
5. Add the next three ingredients. Let cook until heated through before mashing with a fork.
6. Season with salt and black pepper to taste. Set aside.
7. Preheat a griddle pan.
8. Toss together the remaining olive oil and zucchini slices.

9. Season with salt and black pepper to taste.
10. Cook the zucchini slices in the griddle pan until tender. Set aside.
11. Stir together the next three ingredients in a bowl. Set aside.
12. Place the tortilla wraps on a clean working surface.
13. Spread bean puree onto half the tortillas.
14. Top with the zucchini slices.
15. Top with the prepared cheese mixture.
16. Cover with the remaining tortillas.
17. Cook in the griddle pan until crisp.
18. Slice into wedges before serving.

Chorizo and Fried Egg Wraps

Nutritional Information: Calories 340, Fat 20 g.,
Carbohydrates 24 g., Protein 17 g.
Serves 4

Ingredients:

4 chorizos, halved lengthwise
4 whole eggs
4 slices flatbread
2 tbsp. mayonnaise
1 tbsp. capers
4 handfuls arugula

Directions:

1. Place the chorizo halves onto a frying plan.
2. Place the pan on a stove set on low.
3. Gradually increase the heat. Fry the chorizos until they begin to crisp. Set aside.
4. Crack the eggs over the pan and fry them in the leftover oil. Set aside.
5. Place the flatbread on a clean working surface.
6. Spread mayonnaise on the flatbread.
7. Top with the remaining ingredients, followed by the cooked ingredients.
8. Fold to cover the filling. Tuck in the ends.
9. Serve warm.

Refried Bean Quesadillas

Nutritional Information: Calories 487, Fat 18 g.,
Carbohydrates 65 g., Protein 20 g.
Serves 4

Ingredients:

1 tbsp. sunflower oil
1 onion, chopped
2 cloves garlic, chopped
1 tsp. cumin seeds
2 tsp. paprika, smoked
15 oz. pinto beans, canned, rinsed, drained
1 splash water
Salt and black pepper to taste
8 tortilla wraps, warm
3 oz. cheddar cheese, grated
7 oz. tomato salsa
1 handful cilantro leaves
Additional tomato salsa to serve
Sour cream to serve

Directions:

1. Pour the sunflower oil into a skillet.
2. Place the skillet over a stove set on medium.
3. Sauté the next two ingredients for two minutes.
4. Add the cumin. Continue to sauté for one minute.
5. Add the next three ingredients. Let cook until heated through.
6. Mash the beans until smooth.
7. Season with salt and black pepper to taste.
8. Place the tortilla wraps on a clean working surface.
9. Spread prepared bean mixture onto the tortillas.
10. Top with the next three ingredients.

11. Dry the skillet.
12. Fry the prepared tortillas for two minutes each side.
13. Slice into wedges. Serve with salsa and sour cream.

Mediterranean Wraps

Nutritional Information: Calories 436, Fat 26 g.,
Carbohydrates 38 g., Protein 14 g.
Serves 4

Ingredients:

1/4 lb. mushrooms, sliced
1 onion, sliced
1 eggplant, sliced
1 zucchini, sliced
1 bell pepper, sliced
1 tbsp. olive oil
Salt and black pepper to taste

4 tortilla wraps, warm
1/4 c. basil pesto
1/4 c. goat cheese
1 avocado, peeled, pitted, sliced

Directions:

1. Place the first five ingredients in an airtight container.
2. Add the next two ingredients.
3. Seal and shake to coat evenly.
4. Place a skillet over a stove set on medium.
5. Sauté the vegetables for 10 minutes.
6. Place the tortilla wraps on a clean working surface.
7. Spread the next two ingredients on the tortillas.
8. Top with the avocado and sautéed vegetables.
9. Roll and serve.

Cucumber and Avocado Summer Rolls

Nutritional Information: Calories 240, Fat 16 g.,
Carbohydrates 26 g., Protein 5 g.

Serves 4

Ingredients:

> 1/2 tsp. soy sauce
> 1/2 tsp. mustard, Dijon
> 1 tsp. brown sugar
> 1 tbsp. vinegar, rice wine
> 2 tbsp. canola oil
> 1/2 lime, juiced
> 20 rice paper rounds
> 10 lettuce leaves
> 1 bunch mint, leaves only
> 1 bunch basil, leaves only
> 1/2 cucumber, sliced into strips
> 2 avocados, peeled, pitted, diced
> 2 carrots, shredded

Directions:

1. Stir together the first six ingredients in a bowl. Set aside.
2. Dip a rice paper round in warm water until softened.
3. Place the softened round on a towel to drain.
4. Dip another round and place it next to the first round (don't let them touch or they will stick together and tear).
5. Dry the rounds using another towel.
6. Place a lettuce leaf over the dried rounds.
7. Place some mint and basil about a third in from one edge.
8. Top with cucumber, avocadoes and carrots.

9. Carefully lift the edge and roll the rounds over the filling. Tuck in the ends.
10. Repeat until you use up all the ingredients.
11. Slice and serve immediately.

Shrimp and Avocado Summer Rolls

Nutritional Information: Calories 290, Fat 24 g.,
Carbohydrates 19 g., Protein 6 g.
Serves 2

Ingredients:

Rolls

> 12 shrimps, peeled, deveined, tails removed
> 1/8 tsp. salt
> 2 tsp. grapeseed oil
> 4 rice paper wrappers
> 1 avocado, halved, pitted, sliced into 12 portions
> 8 sprigs cilantro
> 4 c. romaine lettuce, shredded

> *Dressing*
> 2 tsp. yellow miso paste
> 2 tbsp. tahini
> 1/2 tsp. sambal oelek
> 2 tbsp. water, warm
> 2 tbsp. lemon juice

Directions:

1. Preheat an oven to 400 degrees F.
2. Arrange the shrimp on a baking sheet in a single layer.
3. Coat evenly with the next two ingredients.
4. Roast for eight minutes. Let cool for a few minutes. Set aside.
5. While waiting, prepare the dressing. To start, stir together the next two ingredients in a bowl.
6. Gradually whisk in the next three ingredients until smooth. Set aside.
7. Dip a rice paper wrapper in warm water until softened.
8. Place the softened wrapper on a clean working surface.

9. Top with three shrimps, three slices avocado, two sprigs cilantro and one c. lettuce.
10. Carefully roll the wrapper to cover the filling. Tuck in the ends.
11. Serve fresh with the prepared dressing.

Summer Chicken Wraps

Nutritional Information: Calories 390, Fat 17 g.,
Carbohydrates 38 g., Protein 26 g.
Serves 4

Ingredients:

4 tortilla wraps, warm
1/2 c. hummus
12 oz. chicken breasts, cooked, sliced into strips
1/4 c. basil, shredded
1/2 c. carrots, shredded
1/2 cucumber, sliced
1 avocado, peeled, pitted, sliced
2 tomatoes, sliced, deseeded
Salt and black pepper to taste

Directions:

1. Place the tortilla wraps on a clean working surface.
2. Spread hummus onto the tortillas.
3. Top with the remaining ingredients.
4. Roll, slice and serve.

Tex-Mex Burrito

Nutritional Information: Calories 611, Fat 38 g.,
Carbohydrates 33 g., Protein 35 g.
Serves 2

Ingredients:

2 tomatoes, halved, seeds scooped out, then chopped
1 red chili, sliced
3 spring onions, chopped
Salt and black pepper to taste
3 oz. milk
4 whole eggs
1 tsp. olive oil
3 oz. cheddar cheese, grated
2 tortilla wraps
Salsa, sour cream and/or guacamole to serve

Directions:

1. Stir together the tomatoes, half the chili and half the onions in a bowl.
2. Season with salt and black pepper to taste.
3. Whisk together the next two ingredients in a separate bowl.
4. Season with salt and black pepper to taste.
5. Pour the olive oil into a skillet.
6. Place the skillet over a stove set on medium.
7. Sauté the remaining chili and onion for a minute.
8. Pour in the egg mixture. Cook to your liking.
9. Turn off the heat. Stir in the cheese.
10. Place the tortilla wraps on a clean working surface.
11. Top with the cooked eggs.
12. Roll and serve with salsa, sour cream and/or guacamole.

Lamb, Lemon and Dill Flatbread

Nutritional Information: Calories 664, Fat 30 g.,
Carbohydrates 37 g., Protein 56
Serves 4

Ingredients:

2 tsp. salt
2 cloves garlic, chopped
1 tbsp. dill, minced
4 tbsp. olive oil
1 lemon, zested, juiced
1 1/2 lbs. lean lamb, trimmed, sliced into chunks
4 slices flatbread

Directions:

1. Puree the first two ingredients into a paste.
2. Pour the paste into a small bowl.
3. Stir in the next three ingredients.
4. Place the lamb in an airtight container.
5. Pour in the prepared marinade.
6. Let marinate refrigerated for at least two hours. Flip over once at the halfway point.
7. Let thaw for 30 minutes before cooking.
8. Preheat the grill to high.
9. Skewer the marinated lamb.
10. Grill for three minutes each side, while basting with any leftover marinade.
11. Grill the flatbread until heated through.
12. Stuff with the prepared meat.
13. Fold to cover the filling.
14. Serve warm.

Kofta Burgers

Nutritional Information: Calories 295, Fat 18 g.,
Carbohydrates 8 g., Protein 26 g.
Serves 8

Ingredients:

1 tbsp. chili sauce
6 tbsp. garam masala
2 1/4 lbs. lamb, minced
1 bunch cilantro, chopped
1 bulb garlic, chopped
2 onions, grated
Salt to taste
8 slices flatbread
Yogurt to taste
1/2 head red cabbage, shredded
1 onion, sliced
4 tomatoes, halved, sliced

Directions:

1. Preheat a grill to high.
2. Using your hands, combine the first seven ingredients in a bowl.
3. Shape the resulting mixture into 16 patties.
4. Grill for five minutes each side.
5. Grill the flatbread until heated through.
6. Place the flatbread on a clean working surface.
7. Spread yogurt onto the flatbread.
8. Top with two grilled patties and remaining ingredients.
9. Fold to cover the filling and serve warm.

Greek Salad Wraps

Nutritional Information: Calories 297, Fat 18 g.,
Carbohydrates 25 g., Protein 10 g.
Serves 2

Ingredients:

2 tortilla wraps, warm
2 tbsp. humus
3 oz. feta cheese
1 cucumber, sliced into spears
1 tomato, chopped
6 kalamata olives, pitted

Directions:

1. Place the tortillas on clean working surface.
2. Spread humus on the tortillas.
3. Top with the remaining ingredients.
4. Roll, slice and serve.

Mexican Chili Bean Tortilla

Nutritional Information: Calories 354, Fat 15 g.,
Carbohydrates 47 g., Protein 11 g.
Serves 8

Ingredients:

1 tbsp. olive oil
2 cloves garlic, chopped
1 onion, chopped
30 oz. kidney beans, canned, drained
1 tsp. paprika, smoked
2 tbsp. cilantro leaves, chopped
5 tbsp. water
1 zucchini, diced
4 tomatoes, sliced
Salt, black pepper and lime juice to taste
8 tortilla wraps, warm
7 oz. sour cream
1 cucumber, sliced into very thin strips
1/2 head iceberg lettuce, shredded

Directions:

1. Pour the oil into a skillet.
2. Place the skillet over a stove set on medium-high.
3. Sauté the next two ingredients for two minutes.
4. Tip in half the beans. Let cook for two minutes.
5. Mash the ingredients together to make a paste.
6. Add the remaining beans and the next six ingredients. Set aside.
7. Place the tortilla wraps on a clean working surface.
8. Top with the prepared bean mixture and remaining ingredients.
9. Roll and serve.

Omelet Burritos with Jack Cheese and Tomato Salsa

Nutritional Information: 614, Fat 44 g., Carbohydrates 20 g., Protein 36 g.

Serves 1

Ingredients:

1 tbsp. butter, clarified
3 whole eggs
Salt and black pepper to taste
1/2 c. Monterey Jack cheese, grated
1/2 c. tomato salsa
3 sprigs cilantro, chopped
1 tortilla wrap, warm

Directions:

1. Place the butter in a skillet.
2. Place the skillet over a stove set on medium.
3. Crack the eggs over the skillet.
4. Cook in the melted butter until almost set.
5. Season with salt and black pepper to taste.
6. Before the eggs set, sprinkle on the Monterey Jack cheese.
7. Spoon salsa onto the center of the eggs.
8. Set the stove to low.
9. Let cook until the cheese melts.
10. Sprinkle on cilantro. Set aside.
11. Place the tortilla wrap on a clean working surface.
12. Top with the prepared omelet.
13. Roll and serve.

Fall Wraps

Crab and Avocado Tostadas

Nutritional Information: Calories 395, Fat 19 g.,
Carbohydrates 27 g., Protein 22 g.
Serves 2

Ingredients:

1 pinch caster sugar
1 onion, sliced into rings
2 limes, juiced
Salt to taste
2 green onions, sliced
7 oz. fresh crabmeat, drained
1 red chili, deseeded, chopped
Black pepper to taste
1 clove garlic, crushed
1 avocado, peeled, pitted, chopped
2 tortilla wraps, warm
Mixed salad leaves to serve
Lime wedges to serve

Directions:

1. Toss together the first two ingredients in a bowl.
2. Add half the lime juice. Toss to combine.
3. Season with salt to taste. Set aside until softened.
4. Toss together the next two ingredients in a separate bowl.
5. Add half the chili. Toss to combine.
6. Season with black pepper to taste. Set aside.
7. Mash together the next two ingredients in a separate bowl.
8. Add the remaining lime juice and chili. Stir to combine.

9. Season with salt and black pepper to taste. Set aside.
10. Place the tortilla wraps on a clean working surface.
11. Top with the salad leaves, prepared avocado mixture, crab mixture and onion mixture.
12. Roll and serve with more salad leaves and lime wedges.

Shrimp Fajitas with Avocado Cream

Nutritional Information: Calories 320, Fat 22 g.,
Carbohydrates 8 g., Protein 23 g.
Serves 2

Ingredients:

1 red chili, deseeded, chopped
1 bunch cilantro, chopped
2 limes, juiced
2 cloves garlic, crushed
1/2 lb. large shrimp, raw, peeled, tails removed
1 avocado, peeled, pitted, chopped
1 tbsp. sour cream
Salt and black pepper to taste
1 tsp. olive oil
1 red pepper, deseeded, sliced
4 tortilla wraps, warm
Additional sour cream to serve
Mixed salad leaves to serve
Lime wedges to serve

Directions:

1. Stir together half the chili, half the cilantro, half the lime juice and half the garlic in an airtight container.
2. Place the shrimp in the container.
3. Let marinate, while you proceed with the next step. Flip over once.
4. Place the avocado in a food processor.
5. Add the sour cream, remaining chili, lime juice and garlic.
6. Season with salt and black pepper to taste.
7. Puree until smooth.
8. Stir in the remaining cilantro. Set aside.
9. Pour the olive oil into a skillet.
10. Sauté the red pepper until softened.

11. Fry the marinated shrimp for two minutes each side. Set aside.
12. Place the tortilla wraps on a clean working surface.
13. Spread sour cream and avocado cream on the tortillas.
14. Top with salad leaves and cooked prawns.
15. Roll and serve with lime wedges.

Steak and Onion Fajitas with Sweet Corn Salsa

Nutritional Information: Calories 594, Fat 23 g.,
Carbohydrates 69 g., Protein 27 g.
Serves 2

Ingredients:

1 avocado, peeled, pitted, chopped
1 lime, juiced
1/2 bunch cilantro, chopped
3 oz. sweet corn
1 tomato, deseeded, chopped
Salt and black pepper to serve
1 tsp. olive oil, garlic-infused
2 onions, sliced into wedges
1 tbsp. fajita seasoning
1/3 lb. beef steak, sliced, fat trimmed
4 tortilla wraps, warm
Shredded lettuce to serve
Sliced jalapenos to serve
Lime wedges to serve

Directions:

1. Mash together the first two ingredients.
2. Stir in half the cilantro.
3. Add the next three ingredients. Stir to combine. Set aside.
4. Pour the olive oil into a skillet.
5. Place the skillet over a stove set on medium.
6. Sauté for eight minutes. Set aside.
7. Rub fajita seasoning on the beef steak.
8. Season with black pepper to taste.
9. Cook for three minutes on each side. Set aside.
10. Place the tortilla wraps on a clean working surface.

11. Spread prepared salsa onto the tortillas.
12. Top with the lettuce, jalapenos and prepared beef steak.
13. Roll and serve with the leftover salsa and lime wedges.

Turkey and Cranberry Roll-Ups

Nutritional Information: Calories 428, Fat 22 g.,
Carbohydrates 31 g., Protein 28 g.
Serves 1

Ingredients:

>   1 tortilla wrap, warm
>   2 tbsp. humus
>   1/4 avocado, peeled, pitted, chopped
>   3 slices turkey breast, cooked, shredded
>   1 tbsp. prepared cranberry sauce

Directions:

1. Place the tortilla wrap on a clean working surface.
2. Spread humus onto the tortillas.
3. Top with remaining ingredients.
4. Roll, slice and serve.

Turkey Veggie Hoisin Wraps

Nutritional Information: Calories 302, Fat 6 g.,
Carbohydrates 31 g., Protein 33 g.
Serves 2

Ingredients:

1/2 lb. turkey, cooked, sliced into strips
4 tbsp. hoisin sauce
2 tortilla wraps
1/4 cucumber, deseeded, shredded
1 handful watercress
4 spring onions, trimmed, shredded

Directions:

1. Preheat a grill to high.
2. Coat the turkey with half the hoisin sauce.
3. Spread the turkey out in a single layer onto a baking dish.
4. Grill until sizzling.
5. Grill the tortillas until heated through.
6. Place the tortilla wraps on a clean working surface.
7. Spread the remaining hoisin sauce onto the tortillas.
8. Top with the remaining ingredients and prepared turkey.
9. Roll, slice and serve.

Pork Tenderloin with Chipotle Sauce and Pickled Red Onions

Nutritional Information: Calories 305, Fat 10 g.,
Carbohydrates 25 g., Protein 31 g.
Serves 4

Ingredients:

1 onion, sliced thinly
2 limes, juiced
2 tsp. oregano, dried
Salt and black pepper to taste
8 cloves garlic, unpeeled
1 onion, sliced thickly
6 plum tomatoes, halved
2 tbsp. chipotle paste
3 tbsp. brown sugar
2 tbsp. chili powder
2 1/4 lbs. pork tenderloin
4 tortilla wraps, warm
Cilantro to serve

Directions:

1. Stir together the first ingredient, half the lime juice and half the oregano in a bowl.
2. Season with salt and black pepper to taste. Set aside.
3. Place the garlic in a skillet.
4. Dry-fry for eight minutes before peeling. Set aside.
5. Preheat the grill to high.
6. Place the next ingredient in a baking dish.
7. Arrange the tomatoes, cut-side up, in the dish.
8. Season with salt and black pepper to taste.
9. Grill for eight minutes. Transfer to a bowl.
10. Stir in the garlic, chipotle paste, remaining lime juice, one tbsp. sugar and one tsp. chili powder.
11. Pour the mixture into a food processor.

12. Puree until smooth. Transfer to a saucepan.
13. Place the saucepan onto a stove set on low.
14. Let cook until heated through. Set aside. Keep warm.
15. Stir together the remaining oregano, sugar and chili powder in a bowl.
16. Season with salt and black pepper to taste.
17. Rub the resulting mixture onto the pork tenderloin.
18. Grill for five minutes each side.
19. Let cool before slicing. Set aside.
20. Place the tortilla wraps on a clean working surface.
21. Spread some of the prepared sauce onto the tortillas.
22. Top with the grilled pork, prepared onions and cilantro.
23. Roll and serve.

Beef and Broad Bean Quesadillas

Nutritional Information: Calories 737, Fat 40 g.,
Carbohydrates 49 g., Protein 49 g.
Serves 4

Ingredients:

5 oz. broad beans, frozen
1 lb. sirloin steaks
1 tbsp. olive oil
Salt and black pepper to taste
8 tortilla wraps, warm
7 oz. cheddar cheese, grated
2 tbsp. cilantro, chopped
1 tomato, chopped
1 jalapeno, chopped
Additional olive oil as needed
Salsa to serve

Directions:

1. Half-fill a skillet with water.
2. Bring the water to a boil.
3. Cook the beans in the boiling water for one minute. Drain and set aside.
4. Coat the steaks with olive oil.
5. Season with salt and black pepper to taste.
6. Place the seasoned steaks on a skillet.
7. Place the skillet over a stove set on high.
8. Cook for three minutes each side.
9. Let cool before slicing.
10. Place the tortilla wraps on a clean working surface.
11. Top half of the tortillas with cheese, cooked steak, boiled beans and the remaining ingredients.
12. Fold the other half to cover the filling. Seal the sides securely.
13. Lightly coat the exposed half with olive oil.

14. Place the tortillas, oil-side down, onto a skillet.
15. Place the skillet over a stove set on high.
16. Cook one side until crisp.
17. Lightly coat the uncooked side with olive oil.
18. Flip over and continue cooking for another two minutes.
19. Slice into wedges and serve with salsa.

Pork Sausage Wraps

Nutritional Information: Calories 351, Fat 19 g.,
Carbohydrates 37 g., Protein 11 g.
Serves 6

Ingredients:

2 tbsp. sunflower oil
6 pork sausages
1 tsp. mustard seeds
1 onion, sliced
Salt and black pepper to taste
6 tortilla wraps, warm
2 tbsp. tomato relish

Directions:

1. Preheat an oven to 400 degrees F.
2. Pour the sunflower oil into a baking pan.
3. Place the pan into the oven.
4. Place the pork sausages into the heated pan.
5. Bake for 10 minutes.
6. Push the pork sausages to the sides.
7. Toss together the next three ingredients.
8. Scatter the resulting mixture onto the center of the pan.
9. Bake for 15 minutes.
10. Let cool for a few minutes.
11. Place the tortilla wraps on a clean working surface.
12. Top with the prepared sausage, onion mixture and tomato relish.
13. Roll and serve warm.

Sweet Potato Falafels with Coleslaw

Nutritional Information: Calories 486, Fat 8 g.,
Carbohydrates 92 g., Protein 16 g.
Serves 4

Ingredients:

Falafels
1 tsp. cumin, ground
2 tsp. cilantro, ground
1/3 c. flour
1 lb. sweet potatoes, cooked, peeled
1/2 lemon, juiced
1 handful cilantro, chopped
2 cloves garlic, chopped
Salt and black pepper to taste
1 tbsp. olive oil
4 slices flatbread
4 tbsp. humus

Coleslaw
1 tbsp. caster sugar
2 tbsp. vinegar, red wine
1/4 white cabbage, shredded
1/4 red cabbage, shredded
1 carrot, grated
1 onion, sliced

Directions:

1. Preheat an oven to 400 degrees F.
2. Mash together the first eight ingredients until smooth.
3. Shape the mixture into 20 balls.
4. Coat a baking sheet with olive oil.
5. Place the balls on a baking sheet.
6. Bake for 15 minutes.

7. Flip over and bake for another 15 minutes.
8. Let cool for a few minutes. Set aside.
9. While waiting, prepare the coleslaw. To start, stir together the first two ingredients in a bowl.
10. Tip in the remaining ingredients. Toss to coat evenly.
11. Let marinate for 15 minutes. Set aside.
12. Place the flatbread on a clean working surface.
13. Spread humus on the flatbread.
14. Top with the coleslaw and falafels.
15. Roll and serve.

Bean Enchiladas

Nutritional Information: Calories 430, Fat 13 g.,
Carbohydrates 60 g., Protein 23 g.
Serves 4

Ingredients:

1 tsp. olive oil
1/2 lb. carrots, grated
2 onions, chopped
3 tsp. chili powder
15 oz. red kidney beans, canned, drained
15 oz. tomatoes, canned, chopped
Salt and black pepper to taste
6 tortilla wraps
3 oz. cheddar cheese, grated
7 oz. yogurt

Directions:

1. Pour the olive oil into a skillet.
2. Place the skillet over a stove set on medium-high.
3. Sauté the next two ingredients until tender.
4. Add the chili powder. Continue to sauté for another minute.
5. Tip in the next two ingredients.
6. Bring the mixture to a boil.
7. Set the stove on low.
8. Let simmer for 10 minutes. Stir occasionally.
9. Turn off the stove.
10. Season with salt and black pepper to taste.
11. Preheat the grill to high.
12. Spread one tbsp. bean chili into a baking dish.
13. Place the tortilla wraps on a clean working surface.
14. Spread bean chili on the tortillas.
15. Roll, seal and place into the baking dish.
16. Spoon the remaining been chili over the tortillas.

17. Stir together the remaining ingredients in a bowl.
18. Season with salt and black pepper to taste.
19. Spoon into the baking dish.
20. Grill until the top is golden.
21. Serve warm.

Burritos with Squash and Feta Cheese

Nutritional Information: Calories 675, Fat 18 g.,
Carbohydrates 93 g., Protein 38 g.
Serves 4

Ingredients:

1 tbsp. vegetable oil
1 onion, chopped
2 cloves garlic, minced
1 tsp. cumin, ground
10 oz. winter squash, cooked
15 oz. black beans, canned, rinsed, drained
10 oz. spinach leaves
Salt and black pepper to taste
4 tortilla wraps, warm
5 oz. feta cheese, crumbled
1/2 c. salsa
Additional salsa to serve

Directions:

1. Pour the vegetable oil into a skillet.
2. Place the skillet over a stove set on medium.
3. Sauté the next three ingredients for five minutes.
4. Tip in the squash. Cook stirring for three minutes.
5. Add the next two ingredients. Continue to cook stirring for five minutes.
6. Season with salt and black pepper to taste. Set aside.
7. Place the tortilla wraps on a clean working surface.
8. Spread the remaining ingredients on the tortillas.
9. Top with the bean mixture.
10. Roll, slice and serve with salsa.

Avocado, Feta and Cabbage Wrap

Nutritional Information: Calories 473, Fat 43 g.,
Carbohydrates 20 g., Protein 8 g.
Serves 1

Ingredients:

1 tortilla wrap, warm
2 tbsp. feta cheese
1/4 c. red cabbage, shredded
1/4 c. watercress
1/4 c. sprouts
1 avocado, peeled, pitted, sliced
Salt, black pepper and lime juice to taste

Directions:

1. Place the tortilla wrap on a clean working surface.
2. Top with the remaining ingredients.
3. Roll, slice and serve.

Roasted Eggplant, Zucchini and Chickpea Wraps

Nutritional Information: Calories 542, Fat 25 g.,
Carbohydrates 69 g., Protein 24 g.
Serves 4

Ingredients:

1 1/2 tsp. lemon juice
1 tbsp. vinegar, balsamic
3 tbsp. olive oil
1 tbsp. oregano leaves, chopped
1 tbsp. thyme leaves, chopped
Vegetable oil as needed
1 zucchini, cubed
1 eggplant, cubed
1 onion, peeled, halved, cut into wedges
1/2 tsp. salt
6 oz. cherry tomatoes, halved
1 cup chickpeas, canned, drained, rinsed
Black pepper to taste
4 tortilla wraps, warmed
4 oz. mozzarella cheese, sliced

Directions:

1. Preheat an oven to 375 degrees F.
2. Whisk together the first two ingredients.
3. Stir in one tbsp. olive oil, one tsp. oregano and one tsp. thyme. Set aside.
4. Lightly coat a baking sheet with vegetable oil.
5. Toss together the next three ingredients with the remaining oregano and thyme.
6. Spread the resulting mixture in a single layer on the oiled baking sheet.
7. Coat with the remaining olive oil.
8. Roast for 30 minutes.
9. Let cool for a few minutes.

10. Transfer the roasted vegetables into a bowl.
11. Stir in the next four ingredients.
12. Pour in the prepared vinaigrette. Toss to coat evenly.
13. Place the tortilla wraps on a clean working surface.
14. Top with mozzarella and the prepared salad.
15. Roll, slice and serve.

Winter Wraps
Hearty Winter Wraps
Nutritional Information: Calories 282, Fat 5 g.,
Carbohydrates 17 g., Protein 41 g.
Serves 1

Ingredients:

> 1/4 tsp. lemon juice
> 1/2 c. arugula
> Salt and black pepper to taste
> 1 tortilla wrap, whole-wheat
> 1/4 tsp. mustard, whole-grain
> 1 tbsp. feta cheese
> 1 tsp. cranberries, dried
> 3 slices turkey, roasted
> 1/4 pear, sliced

Directions:

1. Toss together the first three ingredients in a bowl.
2. Place the tortilla on a clean working surface.
3. Spread mustard on one side.
4. Top the mustard with the feta cheese.
5. Top the feta cheese with the remaining ingredients and prepared arugula.
6. Roll, slice and serve.

Bittersweet Winter Wraps
Nutritional Information: Calories 286, Fat 13 g.,
Carbohydrates 23 g., Protein 18 g.
Serves 1

Ingredients:

> 1 tortilla wrap
> 1/2 c. mustard green micro greens
> 1/2 c. carrot, grated
> 1/2 c. red cabbage, grated
> 1/2 c. mozzarella cheese, grated
> Preferred salad dressing

Directions:

1. Place the tortilla wrap on clean working surface.
2. Top one side with the remaining ingredients.
3. Roll, slice and serve fresh.

Lamb, Tabouli and Hummus Wraps

Nutritional Information: Calories 559, Fat 30 g.,
Carbohydrates 44 g., Protein 26 g.
Serves 4

Ingredients:

2 tsp. olive oil
1 tbsp. oregano, chopped
1 tbsp. lemon juice
1 clove garlic, crushed
3 lamb leg steaks
2 c. tabouli
3/4 c. hummus dip
4 Lebanese bread rounds

Directions:

1. Stir together the first four ingredients in a bowl.
2. Place the lamb in a baking dish.
3. Pour in the prepared mixture.
4. Let marinate refrigerated for 30 minutes. Turn once at the halfway mark.
5. Preheat a barbecue plate.
6. Cook the marinated lamb to your liking.
7. Let sit on a plate while covered with aluminum foil for five minutes.
8. Thinly slice the cooked lamb.
9. Spread the remaining ingredients onto the bread rounds.
10. Top with the sliced lamb.
11. Roll and serve.

Spiced Patty Wraps with Babaganoush
Nutritional Information: Calories 370, Fat 21 g.,
Carbohydrates 18 g., Protein 26 g.
Serves 8

Ingredients:

1 1/2 tbsp. cumin, ground
1/4 c. cilantro leaves, chopped
1/2 c. breadcrumbs
1 1/2 lbs. beef, minced
1 onion, grated
1 whole egg, whisked
2 chilies, deseeded, chopped
Salt and black pepper to taste
1/4 c. vegetable oil
1/2 bunch cilantro leaves, stems removed
1 bunch mint, leaves removed
1 bunch arugula, ends removed
8 slices lavash bread
9 oz. babaganoush
9 oz. char grilled red pepper, chopped

Directions:

1. Place a skillet over a stove set on medium.
2. Cook the cumin for 30 seconds. Stir continuously.
3. Place the cumin in a bowl.
4. Stir in the next seven ingredients.
5. Shape the mixture into 32 patties.
6. Pour 1 tbsp. vegetable oil into the same skillet.
7. Cook a batch of patties for two minutes per side.
8. Place the cooked patties on a paper towel to drain.
9. Repeat until you use up all the oil and patties.
10. Toss together the next three ingredients in a bowl.

11. Place the bread on a clean working surface.
12. Spread babaganoush on each slice.
13. Top with the arugula mixture, followed by the red pepper and four patties.
14. Roll, slice and serve.

Chicken and Rice Wraps

Nutritional Information: Calories 592, Fat 23 g.,
Carbohydrates 67 g., Protein 26 g.
Serves 6

Ingredients:

6 tortilla wraps
2 tbsp. vegetable oil
2 cloves garlic, chopped
1 brown onion, diced
1/2 c. cashews
1/2 tsp. turmeric, ground
1 tsp. cumin, ground
1 c. white rice
1 1/2 c. chicken stock
1 tbsp. curry paste
1 lb. chicken thigh fillets, fat trimmed, diced
5 oz. baby spinach
1/4 c. mango chutney
1/2 c. Greek yogurt

Directions:

1. Preheat an oven to 350 degrees F.
2. Pour 1 tbsp. vegetable oil into a skillet.
3. Place the skillet over a stove set on medium.
4. Sauté the next two ingredients for two minutes.
5. Add the cashews. Continue to sauté for another two minutes.
6. Stir in the next three ingredients.
7. Pour in the stock. Stir to combine.
8. Set the stove on high.
9. Bring the mixture to a boil. Stir occasionally.
10. Set the stove to low.
11. Let simmer covered for 12 minutes. Do not stir.
12. Turn off the stove.

13. Let sit covered for 10 minutes.
14. While waiting, wrap the tortillas in aluminum foil.
15. Bake the tortillas for 10 minutes.
16. Pour the remaining vegetable oil into a saucepan.
17. Place the saucepan over a stove set on medium.
18. Cook the curry paste for one minute. Stir continuously.
19. Sauté the chicken in the heated paste for five minutes.
20. Place the warmed tortillas on a clean working surface.
21. Top with the prepared rice, chicken and remaining ingredients.
22. Roll and serve warm.

Speedy Pesto Wraps

Nutritional Information: Calories 288, Fat 13 g.,
Carbohydrates 23 g., Protein 22 g.
Serves 4

Ingredients:

> 1/4 c. pesto sauce, low-fat
> 1/4 c. cream cheese, low-fat, softened
> 4 tortilla wraps
> 8 oz. turkey breast, smoked, sliced
> 1/2 c. tomatoes, chopped
> 2 c. lettuce, shredded

Directions:

1. Stir together the first two ingredients in a bowl.
2. Place the tortillas on a clean working surface.
3. Spread the prepared mixture over one side.
4. Top with the remaining ingredients.
5. Roll and serve.

Veggie Wraps with Grilled Cheese

Nutritional Information: Calories 487, Fat 38 g.,
Carbohydrates 25 g., Protein 14 g.
Serves 4

Ingredients:

4 tortilla wraps
4 tbsp. butter, softened
1 tsp. chipotle pepper in adobo sauce, diced
4 tbsp. mayonnaise, light
6 oz. Swiss cheese, sliced
Filling
2 tsp. olive oil
1/2 c. carrots, shredded
1 1/2 c. broccoli slaw
6 green onions, sliced

Directions:

1. Prepare the filling. To start, pour the olive oil into a skillet.
2. Sauté the remaining ingredients until tender. Set aside.
3. Place the tortillas on a clean working surface.
4. Spread butter on one side of each tortilla.
5. Stir together the next two ingredients.
6. Spread the resulting mixture over the other side of the tortillas.
7. Top the mayonnaise-side with Swiss cheese and the prepared filling.
8. Fold to cover the filling.
9. Place a skillet over a stove set on medium.
10. Cook the tortillas for five minutes each side.
    a. Or Preheat a Panini maker.
    b. Cook the tortillas for three minutes.
11. Serve immediately.

Cheesy Tortilla Wraps

Nutritional Information: Calories 248, Fat 9 g.,
Carbohydrates 34 g., Protein 10 g.
Serves 2

Ingredients:

4 tortilla wraps
1 tbsp. jalapenos, chopped
3 oz. cheddar cheese, grated
1 handful cilantro, chopped
1 red pepper, roasted

Directions:

1. Place two tortillas on a grill pan.
2. Top with the remaining ingredients.
3. Cover with the remaining tortillas.
4. Grill for three minutes.
5. Flip over. Continue to grill for another three minutes.
6. Slice into wedges.
7. Serve warm.

Hot Leg of Lamb Wraps

Nutritional Information: Calories 661, Fat 29 g.,
Carbohydrates 67 g., Protein 30 g.
Serves 4

Ingredients:

5 peppadew peppers
4 lamb leg steaks
1 tsp. cumin, ground
2 tsp. olive oil
Salt and black pepper to taste
1 tbsp. sugar
3 tbsp. vinegar, white wine
14 oz. white cabbage, sliced
2 spring onions, sliced
2 carrots, grated
3 tbsp. mayonnaise
4 slices flatbread, warm

Directions:

1. Preheat a griddle.
2. Slice two peppadew peppers. Set aside.
3. Coat the steaks with the next three ingredients.
4. Cook in the griddle for four minutes each side.
5. Trim the excess fat off the steaks. Slice thinly. Set aside.
6. Stir together the next two ingredients.
7. Stir in the next three ingredients.
8. Season with salt and black pepper to taste. Set aside.
9. Puree the whole peppers in a food processor.
10. Add the mayonnaise. Puree until smooth.
11. Place the flatbread on a clean working surface.

12. Top with a heap of prepared salad and sliced steak.
13. Spoon the mayonnaise mixture over the steak layer.
14. Top with sliced peppers.
15. Roll, slice and serve.

Melting Chili Bean Wraps

Nutritional Information: Calories 509, Fat 9 g.,
Carbohydrates 89 g., Protein 24 g.
Serves 2

Ingredients:

15 oz. mixed beans in chili sauce
1 handful cherry tomatoes, halved
4 tortilla wraps
2 handfuls cheddar cheese, grated
Guacamole to serve

Directions:

1. Preheat a grill to high.
2. Pour the beans into a saucepan.
3. Place the pan over a stove set on medium.
4. Add the tomatoes. Cook stirring for five minutes.
5. Place the tortillas on a clean working surface.
6. Top with the prepared bean mixture and cheddar cheese.
7. Roll and place on a baking sheet.
8. Grill for three minutes.
9. Slice and serve with guacamole.

Cheese and Chili Melts

Nutritional Information: Calories 298, Fat 18 g.,
Carbohydrates 24 g., Protein 12 g.
Serves 8

Ingredients:

9 oz. cheddar cheese, grated
1/2 bunch cilantro leaves, chopped
1 red chili, deseeded, chopped
4 tomatoes, chopped
Salt and black pepper to taste
8 tortilla wraps, warm
Vegetable oil as needed

Directions:

1. Stir together the first five ingredients in a bowl.
2. Place the tortillas on a clean working surface.
3. Top with the prepared cheese mixture.
4. Fold and seal the edges tightly.
5. Coat lightly with vegetable oil.
6. Cook the tortillas oil-side down until golden.
7. Coat the uncooked side with vegetable oil.
8. Flip over and continue to cook until golden.
9. Slice and serve warm.

Spicy Vegetable Wraps

Nutritional Information: Calories 298, Fat 5 g.,
Carbohydrates 54 g., Protein 12 g.
Serves 4

Ingredients:

2/3 lb. sweet potatoes, peeled, cubed
1/2 tsp. chili flakes, dried
2 tbsp. curry paste
15 oz. chickpeas, canned, drained
15 oz. plum tomatoes, canned, peeled
3 oz. baby spinach
2 tbsp. cilantro, chopped
Salt and black pepper to taste
4 slices flatbread
4 tbsp. Greek yogurt

Directions:

1. Preheat a grill to medium.
2. Boil the sweet potatoes until tender. Drain. Set aside.
3. Stir together the next four ingredients in a saucepan.
4. Bring the mixture to a boil.
5. Let simmer for five minutes.
6. Stir in the sweet potatoes and spinach. Let cook for one minute.
7. Stir in the next two ingredients.
8. Grill the flatbread for 30 seconds each side.
9. Spread yogurt onto the grilled bread.
10. Top with the prepared filling.
11. Fold in half before serving.

Cajun Turkey Wraps with Sweet Corn Salsa

Nutritional Information: Calories 574, Fat 14 g.,
Carbohydrates 75 g., Protein 42 g.
Serves 4

Ingredients:

4 turkey breast steaks
1 tbsp. Cajun spice mix
1 tbsp. olive oil
10 oz. sweet corn, canned, rinsed, drained
1/2 lime, zested and juiced
1 red chili, deseeded, chopped
8 tortilla wraps, warm
5 oz. sour cream

Directions:

1. Coat the turkey with the spice mix.
2. Pour the olive oil into a skillet.
3. Cook the turkey for four minutes each side.
4. Let cool before slicing. Set aside.
5. Stir together the next three ingredients in a bowl.
6. Place the tortillas on a clean working surface.
7. Spread sour cream onto the tortillas.
8. Top with the sliced turkey and prepared salsa.
9. Roll and serve.

Conclusion

First and foremost, I would like to express my most heartfelt thanks for purchasing this book! I deeply appreciate your business and hope you enjoyed reading about and trying our recipes.

Don't depend on the lunch lady to keep you healthy. Just because you're eating in the office, doesn't mean that you can't eat well, and dining out every day may not only be bad for your healthy, but also your wallet.

And there's no need to fear looking like a second-grader with a Peanut Butter and Jelly sandwich, now that you have the *Wrap of the Week Cookbook*.

With a combination of 52 delicious, nutritious and easy-to-prepare wrap recipes, you'll be packing a new, convenient, flavorful and money-saving meal for every week of the year. The book's emphasis on seasonal ingredients will also allow you to purchase ingredients during their peak season, which means that they will not only be fresher, but also relatively cheaper. Whether you're a busy office worker, budget-conscious student or lunch-packing mother, I hope you've enjoyed it!

Lucy Fast

Check out some of Lucy's other books in her healthy Paleo Diet Solution Series!!

http://www.amazon.com/dp/B00IIHKA84

http://www.amazon.com/dp/B00J1UOLMI

http://www.amazon.com/dp/B00IJ17FLO

http://www.amazon.com/dp/B00ICYALXC

http://www.amazon.com/dp/B00HH1GBLC

http://www.amazon.com/dp/B00J1TU18C

http://www.amazon.com/dp/B00JOS53H4

Made in the USA
Columbia, SC
22 November 2024